Executing
Innovation

Pocket Mentor Series

The *Pocket Mentor* Series offers immediate solutions to common challenges managers face on the job every day. Each book in the series is packed with handy tools, self-tests, and real-life examples to help you identify your strengths and weaknesses and hone critical skills. Whether you're at your desk, in a meeting, or on the road, these portable guides enable you to tackle the daily demands of your work with greater speed, savvy, and effectiveness.

Books in the series:

Leading Teams
Running Meetings
Managing Time
Managing Projects
Coaching People
Giving Feedback
Leading People
Negotiating Outcomes
Writing for Business
Giving Presentations
Understanding Finance
Dismissing an Employee
Creating a Business Plan

Managing Stress
Delegating Work
Shaping Your Career
Persuading People
Managing Crises
Managing Up
Becoming a New Manager
Managing Difficult Interactions
Hiring an Employee
Making Decisions
Managing Diversity
Executing Innovation

Executing Innovation

Innovation

Expert Solutions to
Everyday Challenges

Harvard Business Press

Boston, Massachusetts

No part of this publication may be reproduced, stored in or introduced into a re-
trieval system, or transmitted, in any form, or by any means (electronic, mechanical,
photocopying, recording, or otherwise), without the prior permission of the pub-
lisher. Requests for permission should be directed to permissions@hbsp.harvard.edu,
or mailed to Permissions, Harvard Business School Publishing, 60 Harvard Way,
Boston, Massachusetts 02163.

Library of Congress Cataloging-in-Publication Data

Executing innovation : expert solutions to everyday challenges.
    p. cm. — (Pocket mentor series)
  Includes bibliographical references and index.
  ISBN 978-1-4221-2881-7 (pbk. : alk. paper)
  1. Technological innovations. 2. Creative ability in business. I. Harvard
Business Press.
  HD45.E96 2009
  658.4'063—dc22

                                                              2008039446

The paper used in this publication meets the requirements of the American National
Standard for Permanence of Paper for Publications and Documents in Libraries and
Archives Z39.48-1992.

Contents

Tips and Tools   63

Mentor's Message: Why Executing Innovation Matters

To stay competitive, companies must continually come up with innovative new products, services, and ways of doing business (such as reducing error rates or understanding customers better). And all that innovation calls for creative thinking. But creativity is just the first step to successful innovation: if fresh ideas aren't executed—if they aren't turned into *actual* new offerings or business processes—then they're of little use to an organization.

Executing innovation isn't easy. An innovator can run into numerous roadblocks, including resistance to his or her new idea and a loss of momentum as practical challenges eat away at the initial enthusiasm for the idea. This guide shows you how to navigate these obstacles so your exciting idea becomes far more than just an idea—and so it generates measurable value for your organization.

Kumar Nochur, Mentor

Kumar Nochur is a consultant and educator with over twenty years of experience in the field of implementing innovation. He has taught business strategy, innovation, and technology management courses at Boston University and the University of Melbourne. He has worked with such industry leaders as 3M, AT&T (Bell Labs), General Electric, Gillette, Procter & Gamble, Johnson & Johnson, and National Semiconductor to improve their innovation practices. Dr. Nochur leads courses and workshops on topics such as *Skills for Innovators* and *Managing Innovation*. He is also a frequent speaker at conferences on innovation, new product development, and knowledge management. Dr. Nochur received a PhD in the management of technological innovation from the Sloan School of Management at MIT. He is the founder of Vidya, Inc.

Executing Innovation: The Basics

Why Innovate?

TODAY'S BUSINESS environment is rapidly changing. New technologies, governmental regulations, and global market conditions are forcing companies to quickly develop new products and differentiate their service offerings while increasing productivity and cost efficiency. To maintain their competitive advantage, companies need to innovate.

When you hear the word *innovation*, you may think of a technology-driven service such as online shopping, or a groundbreaking product such as the smart mobile phone. However, innovation comes in many forms. For example, consider a new process for efficiently sharing information and internal expertise within a software development firm with offices in New York and Berlin. Employees who don't know each other could communicate client information and revise product specifications in real time. This innovative process may not involve any new technology or result in a new product, but it could give the company significant competitive advantage by increasing the knowledge base of its employees and improving customer service.

INNOVATION *n* **1:** A new product, service, or way of doing business that gives an organization a competitive advantage

---

However, creative ideas for new products, services, and business processes don't necessarily become innovations. Innovation occurs only when novel ideas have been developed, packaged, positioned, promoted, and implemented. Successful innovators thus pick up where the creative-thinking process leaves off. They take a fresh idea and apply it to a real-life problem, resulting in a new product, service, or process that gains widespread use. By understanding types of innovators and the steps toward executing an innovation, you can begin learning more about how to turn creative ideas into valuable new products, services, or processes in your own organization.

Types of innovators

New ideas become reality through the work of innovators. Innovators, however, rarely work alone. There are different types of innovators, each of whom plays a unique role in the innovation process:

- **Idea generators conceive ideas.** Creative ideas can spring up anywhere in the organization, not just in the R&D function, which is traditionally seen as the source for new ideas.

- **Idea facilitators help create the conditions necessary to execute innovations.** They provide the information, resources, and support to help a novel idea be transformed into an actual product, service, or new process.

- **Innovation champions assume the responsibility for executing ideas.** The champion need not be the creator of the idea, but he or she has the enthusiasm and commitment necessary to lead the process of promoting and implementing it.

Research suggests that a committed champion is *most* critical to the successful execution of an idea—especially if the idea represents a radical innovation opportunity or if the need for it is not generally recognized. A powerful idea can remain dormant in a company for years because nobody assumes responsibility for carrying it out. An innovation champion has the know-how, energy, daring, dedication, and perseverance that are needed to turn such an idea into reality. While many people can generate creative ideas or provide an environment that encourages innovation, few actually commit to putting ideas into action.

"Creativity is thinking up new things. Innovation is doing new things."
—Theodore Levitt

Perhaps few people choose to take on this challenge because innovation champions frequently encounter resistance. Consider the development of the airplane. The innovators whose vision turned the idea of human flight into a reality did so in spite of skeptics who could not imagine how people would ever travel by air. Those innovators certainly proved the skeptics wrong!

Spotlight on innovation champions

If you choose to champion an idea, consider your level of commitment to the idea and whether you think it will work. The checklist "Could you be an innovation champion?" in the "Tools for Executing Innovation" section of this book helps you determine whether this role is for you.

Seven steps to executing an innovation

Being ready and willing to champion an idea means you also need to be ready for the hard work of carrying it out. This book lays out a seven-step process for your execution:

1. **Develop an inspiring vision of your innovation.** Capture your vision in a statement that describes your idea and helps rally support for it.

2. **Identify stakeholders.** Identify the people who will be affected by your innovation or who control the resources you need to implement it. Consider the criteria they will use to evaluate your idea so you can address their interests and concerns early in the process.

3. **Cultivate an informal support network.** You will need people to provide technical, political, financial, and other forms of support to make your idea a reality. In the early stages, you'll need informal supporters whom you can call on as needed.

4. **Build a business case.** The business case establishes the worth of your idea in terms of benefits to your customers and returns to your company. You will use the business case to generate buy-in and support for your idea.

5. **Communicate with stakeholders.** Demonstrate to people within and outside of your organization the merits of your idea to get the resources and support you need.

6. **Manage any resistance.** Inevitably, some people will oppose your idea. You will have to work to manage their concerns so they don't derail your project.

7. **Stay passionate about your innovation.** Innovation takes time. To sustain momentum for your project, you'll have to maintain your enthusiasm.

The steps taken to execute an innovation may not follow in the exact order listed. You can pursue some steps in parallel or in a different sequence, depending on the specifics of your situation.

"Every organization—not just business—needs one core competence: innovation."
    —Peter Drucker

Step 1: Develop an Inspiring Vision

CONSIDER THE following situation:

> As a product manager in a company making outdoor gear, you notice that customers are increasingly interested in extreme sports, an area that your company is not currently serving. Glancing through magazines that serve this trendy market, you come up with an idea for a line of clothing using high-tech new materials that would appeal to extreme sports enthusiasts. Although this market is relatively small, you think it will grow into a bigger segment in the next few years. Your concern is that management might not be receptive to the idea because it currently has limited market potential.

How would you get people excited about this idea? The starting point for success as an innovation champion is a powerful vision—a picture in your mind's eye of the completely successful realization of your idea.

Creating a vision statement

Since your vision is inside your head, you'll need a means of communicating it to others. A clear vision statement functions as a mechanism for getting your idea out in the world. A vision statement achieves the following:

- **It expresses in an exciting way the ideal outcome you'd like to achieve.** A vision statement should provide a succinct, big-picture view of the positive changes that will occur once the idea is executed.

- **It motivates and inspires people to take action in the right direction.** Ideally, a vision statement addresses goals or a common cause that your audience can identify with. By painting a picture that appeals directly to your audience's values, you'll be more likely to inspire them to commit to your vision.

"The creative process does not end with an idea; it starts with one. Creative ideas are just the first step in a long process of bringing thoughts into reality."
—Alex Osborn

Once you identify an idea, product, or project that you believe is worth pursuing, write down the answers to the following questions:

- What is the innovation?

- Do you have a name for the idea or project?

- What is your role? For example, are you the idea generator? The champion? Or do you have some other role?

- What benefits make the innovation worth pursuing? How will it affect customers, end users, or other beneficiaries?

What Would YOU Do?

Cleaning Up at CleanCo

M ARTIN IS A PROJECT manager at CleanCo, a small engineering firm that specializes in designing cleanup strategies for contaminated properties. Recently, Martin has noticed that his clients seem eager to get rid of these properties. He is also aware of new land-use policies that push companies to reuse industrial sites instead of building their facilities on pristine land. Martin sees an opportunity in the real estate business for CleanCo. He thinks that his company could buy contaminated properties at a significantly reduced price, do the site cleanup, and resell them at a huge profit. He knows the president of the company is eager to grow the business in a new direction. Martin wants to approach her with his idea right away, since he'd like to persuade her to get into the business before competitors do. But as this is the first time he's come up with such an idea, he's not sure whether that's the best next step.

What would YOU do? The mentors will suggest a solution in *What You COULD Do.*

Next, you may want to close your eyes and imagine a time in the future when the innovation has been successfully carried out. Focus on the ideal outcome, not on how you got there. Then jot down what you're seeing in your mind's eye. You may want to do this exercise frequently to help develop a clear image of your idea.

Steps for Developing Your Vision

1. **Find a relaxing place to think.**
   Look for a quiet place where you can spend some time undisturbed. Sit down, relax, and close your eyes.

2. **Focus on your idea.**
   Think of a time in the future when the innovation has been successfully implemented. Imagine how your idea has unfolded. In a best-case scenario, what does your innovation look like? How are people responding to your idea? How has your idea impacted your company?

3. **Shift your focus to yourself.**
   Next, imagine what it would feel like to experience the rewards of a successful execution. Again, focus on the best-case scenario. What does success look like? How do you feel? Think about the outcome, not about how you achieved it.

4. **Record your vision.**
   After about five minutes of visualizing, record your vision in whatever way you think is best. You might sketch a picture, build a model, or write a paragraph to describe your vision. See the worksheet for crafting a vision statement for help in capturing your vision on paper.

5. **Replay your vision regularly.**

   On a regular basis, replay the vision in your mind. Regular reflection will help to keep you focused on the creative execution of your idea—and help you stay motivated when you face inevitable obstacles or setbacks.

6. **Convey your vision with excitement and enthusiasm.**

   Once you can describe your vision, it is time to test it. Telling people about your idea with excitement and enthusiasm will help to attract them to it. Ask colleagues and friends to react to your idea and help you revise your vision to make it even more compelling and clear.

To continue the earlier example, you might generate the following preliminary vision statement:

> *We have an opportunity to leverage our strong brand in developing a new market—extreme sports—that will become a major segment in the next five years. By applying our expertise with low-weight, high-tech composites to make a new line of clothing for this market, we can gain greater buzz for our company. I see the Omega line of clothing becoming the preferred choice of extreme sports customers. Our tagline can be, "Omega Xtreme—Designed for Your Omega Xperience!" This market will pay premium prices, so we will have a greater profit margin on our sales. The experience we gain with this high-end emerging market will help us spin off related new products at lower cost to other segments we already serve.*

The table "How good is your vision statement?" in the "Tools for Executing Innovation" section of this book helps you make sure your statement has all the right qualities.

Testing and refining your vision

Once you write down your preliminary vision statement, you are ready to test and refine it. Be sure to:

- **Ask for feedback and take notes.** Assemble a few colleagues, friends, or other people you trust and respect, and ask them to react to your idea from the perspective of your intended audience. Make note of the questions they ask, and listen attentively to their suggestions.

- **Modify your initial idea with the feedback you receive.** Constructing your vision is an iterative process. The feedback you receive will give you the opportunity to improve on your initial vision, retest it, and make it more and more compelling.

- **Be patient.** While some innovators instantly have clear visions of what they'd like to create, others build their vision over a period of time, as the idea and its impact evolve. You will likely fine-tune your vision several times before you feel ready to communicate it to a broader audience.

Your goal is to have a solid vision statement at the end of this process—but it doesn't have to be perfect. After identifying your stakeholders and developing your business case, you will likely work with your supporters to refine this vision statement further.

What You COULD Do.

Remember Martin's question about how best to present his new idea?

Here's what the mentor suggests:

Martin has a good idea and is enthusiastic about pursuing it. He should not rush to seek the president's support, however. He should first take the time to develop a compelling vision statement, identify his key stakeholders, and consider the criteria they might use to evaluate his idea. He should then seek feedback from his peers.

For example, Martin should approach his colleagues in the engineering department about the costs and risks of the cleanup process. He should also consult with regulatory and legal specialists about how ownership of the contaminated properties would be transferred. As he cultivates his informal support network, he would do well to identify a sponsor who understands the politics of his organization to help him promote his idea. After he builds peer support for his idea and gathers sufficient business information to lend credibility to his case, he will be ready to communicate his idea to the president.

Step 2: Identify Stakeholders

STAKEHOLDERS ARE THE KEY parties who will be affected by your innovation. They can facilitate the successful execution of your vision—or they can sabotage it. As you develop your idea, be sure to consider their needs and address their concerns.

While you may not communicate with all your stakeholders at the outset of your project, you should be aware of them so you can address their needs during your planning stage. Later in the process, you'll seek their support. The work you do now will help you influence them later.

Naming key parties

Who are your key stakeholders? They can be both internal and external to your organization, and most likely will include the following:

- **Customers.** Potential customers or end users, whether internal or external, are the ultimate reason for developing new products, processes, and services. In most instances, an innovation directly affects them. For example, your idea could reduce the price they pay for a service they already buy or could provide them with a new and better product to purchase.

- **Investors.** This group includes all of the people who control the necessary resources, such as money, staffing, and equipment, for you to successfully implement your idea. They could be at any level—from company executives, such as the chief financial officer, to department or division heads—depending on your company's managerial structure.

- **Intermediaries.** These are the people who are involved with the development and implementation of your innovation in some fashion. They appear somewhere in the pipeline between you and the end users or customers of the innovation. They could include people in internal departments such as finance, manufacturing, or sales, as well as external parties such as suppliers and distributors.

"The force of any idea originates in the essential needs, perceived preferences, and unconscious expectations of the people it is intended to serve."
—Michael E. Gerber

You may also have other stakeholders who are less visible than those listed above. While these secondary stakeholders are more difficult to identify, do consider them when planning to move forward with your idea. This group may include the following:

- People within and outside your organization whose reputations, expertise, or track records enable them to influence decision makers

- Anyone who stands to gain or lose something once your idea is implemented

- People who are staunch supporters of the status quo, possibly because of their role in creating the status quo

- Other people with innovative ideas who may be competing for attention or resources

Understanding stakeholders' concerns

By considering stakeholder concerns early, you'll be better prepared to garner support when you need it, and better able to anticipate resistance. For example, if you propose changing the inventory tracking system for your company, you could anticipate that the distribution department might have to work overtime to learn the new system while keeping up with current orders. Identify a way to make the situation better for the workers, such as allowing them extra compensation for the overtime. Then approach the distribution team members with your idea.

A common mistake innovators make is to focus on the features of the innovation and to spend little time identifying the benefits the idea will have for each stakeholder. When it comes time for you to present your idea to others, you stand a better chance of succeeding if you've thought about the innovation from the perspective of your stakeholders. What would they be most interested in knowing about? What might concern them about your idea? Identifying these issues early will help you focus on the most relevant details of your idea when you meet with a stakeholder.

Tip: Connect your innovation with each stakeholder's needs, wants, and priorities. When you are seeking stakeholder support, tailor your presentation to address the individual interests of your audience.

Each group of stakeholders will have its own interests and agenda, and will evaluate your idea using different criteria. The table "Stakeholders' evaluation criteria" shows a list of potential criteria to consider for each key stakeholder group.

Stakeholders' evaluation criteria

Stakeholder group	Potential evaluation criteria
Customers	• Do we need or want the innovation? • How significant are its benefits? • How is your idea better than what we have now? • Is the added benefit worth the price? • Is it easy to use and derive benefits from? • What are the risks we could face if your innovation does not deliver as expected?
Internal investors	• What is the return on investment? • What are the nonfinancial benefits/rewards? • Is it the best use of our resources? • How well does it meet the goals, strategies, and culture of our organization? • What are the odds of failure? • What are the consequences of failure?
Intermediaries	• What does this innovation require from us? • How does the idea impact our power, status, or work schedule? • How does this idea benefit our role or function?

As you gather information and develop your idea, list the potential stakeholders and their likely concerns. You may want to approach some stakeholders early for advice, to get them to buy into your idea. Ask your various supporters to help identify potential concerns and develop strategies for addressing them.

Steps for Building Support for Your Idea

1. **Seek input and advice.**

   As you develop your idea, ask for input from trusted friends and colleagues. Don't try to sell your idea at this point. Instead, ask them to identify potential problems and flaws in your thinking. Ask them to challenge your assumptions and suggest ways to improve your idea. Revise your idea on the basis of the feedback you receive.

2. **Identify stakeholders.**

   Consider who will be affected by your idea and who controls the resources you will need to execute it. Ask yourself how these people might respond to your idea. Before you meet with them, anticipate their concerns and be prepared to answer their questions. The person you choose as your sponsor should be able to offer insights about the decision makers and stakeholders you'll need to win over.

3. **Develop a communication strategy.**

   After you have explored the details of your project and feel ready to seek outside support, develop a strategy for influencing stakeholders. Work with your sponsor or other trusted advisers to decide how and when to approach each person. For some, an informal meeting may suffice. For others, a detailed presentation may be more appropriate. Make sure to identify your objectives for speaking with each stakeholder so that you know what you are asking for before you meet with them.

4. **Meet with important stakeholders.**

   Implement the communication strategy you developed. Present your ideas and ask for input and support. Revise your communication strategy on the basis of the feedback you receive in early meetings. If you meet with strong resistance, take a step back to understand its causes so that you can address it properly.

5. **Keep supporters informed of your progress.**

   Make sure to keep your sponsor and key stakeholders informed of your progress. You want your project to stay in the forefront of your supporters' minds so they will continue to view it as important and relevant.

Step 3: Cultivate Your Support Network

I T'S RARE THAT ONE person can take an idea from concept to completion. Typically, no one person controls all of the information, expertise, and resources required to bring an idea to fruition. Executing an innovative idea requires the support and assistance of many people.

Contacting people whom you already know and rely on in other areas of your career is a good place to start. Someone who knows you and respects your work is more likely to take the time to help you with your project than someone who doesn't know you and isn't sure of your capabilities.

Getting early buy-in

While you are probably excited about your idea and want to get started immediately, it is preferable to take the time to build the support you need. If you approach someone and say, "I have a great idea for a new product, and I would like you to support it. I will need your help to get financial resources and people to work on development and implementation," you will likely overwhelm the person and fail to get his or her assistance.

Rather, as you develop your idea, ask people you trust for small things such as advice and input on your vision statement. You could say, "I have a really interesting idea and would appreciate your advice. Do you have a few minutes to discuss it?" Use the feedback you generate to refine and shape your idea—and position it in terms of benefits to others. Then go back to the most helpful individuals or those who were most enthusiastic, and gradually ask them for larger commitments of time or resources.

"Innovation . . . is seldom the product of a single individual's intellectual brilliance. Innovation is the product of the connections between individuals and their ideas."
—Gary Hamel

As people get more involved in your project, they may volunteer to take on more responsibility for its execution. Even if some people do nothing more than provide initial advice, by asking for their opinions early, you engage them in the development of the idea and thereby establish connections that could help you down the road. Engaging others early also gives them a sense of ownership in the idea that often leads to the support and commitment you'll need to make your idea a reality.

Assigning key roles

As you refine your idea and widen your circle of support, you'll begin to think about the kinds of people whose assistance you'll need to get concrete backing for your idea. Research has shown that the help of certain people can greatly increase the probability of success with innovation projects. These roles are:

- **Sponsor.** A sponsor is usually a senior person in an organization in a position of power. He or she often provides help with execution problems and ways to present an idea more effectively to management. This individual frequently works behind the scenes to support the venture by helping to acquire necessary resources and by preventing the idea from being killed prematurely.

- **Gatekeeper.** A gatekeeper is usually an expert in a functional area or subject, such as R&D, manufacturing, or sales. This person is up-to-date in knowledge of his or her field and can serve as a useful sounding board and information resource as you develop your idea and build a business case to support it. Drawing on extensive contacts within and outside your organization, he or she can also connect you with other people who can help you with information, expertise, or other resources.

- **Opinion leader.** An opinion leader is well respected for his or her expertise, judgment, and insights. This is an individual whom people frequently consult before making a decision. An opinion leader's endorsement lends credibility to your venture and helps accelerate acceptance of your new idea. On the flip side, if an opinion leader criticizes your idea, he or she can erode its support quickly. Therefore, it's critical to identify opinion leaders to support your idea early on.

These roles are not formally designated job titles or responsibilities. Sometimes the same individual may play more than one role. For example, the gatekeeper may also be your opinion leader.

Gathering your network members

People in your network will have different levels of responsibility and commitment to your project. For example, you may meet with a high-level sponsor only once in a while to ask for advice or guidance on how to handle large execution issues. On the other hand, you may ask a core group of people with technical expertise and marketing knowledge to meet weekly or even daily to discuss the details of your idea and to move the project forward.

The number of people in your support network will probably vary according to the size of your project and your organization. The network gradually expands as the champion identifies additional needed resources and as people get excited about the idea and volunteer to help implement it.

Typically, successful innovators first build a support network of peers and colleagues, and then seek support at higher levels. The timing for approaching upper-level executives can be tricky. This is an area where your sponsor's political savvy and knowledge of how your company operates is particularly useful. While it's important to get upper management's approval in a timely fashion, seeking their support before you have a strategy for influencing them could jeopardize your project.

Innovators frequently focus on influencing the decision makers and the people who will be directly affected by the innovation. They forget to look for support from opinion leaders and customers. These groups can have enormous influence on decision makers and should be considered when you are developing your communication or execution strategy.

Tip: While gathering feedback on your idea, don't forget to talk with external sources, such as important customers and opinion leaders.

Waiting too long to approach key people in upper management can be as problematic as approaching them too early. It is essential to get some key decision makers on board relatively quickly. That way, you don't proceed with a project without knowing whether you'll be able to get the resources you need. Ask your sponsor to help you develop a strategy for approaching influential people and stakeholders at the appropriate time.

Step 4: Build Your Business Case

ONCE YOU'VE ASSEMBLED your support network and identified your stakeholders, you're ready to start building a business case for your idea. This task involves creative thinking about how the innovation could unfold, and analytical thinking about how the idea will affect your organization, its employees and customers, and other stakeholders. The thinking and debate that go into the creation of the business case are as important as the final document you produce.

The business case for an innovative idea contains the information you'll need to influence people to support your idea. To get the approval and resources you need to succeed, you have to demonstrate to management and other stakeholders the merits of your idea.

For example, you may believe that your proposed innovation will reduce the time it takes to complete a weekly status report for your consulting clients. As you gather more information, you might be able to quantify the time it would save and estimate how that time savings will translate into increased profits for your company.

Getting started

Create a preliminary outline to use as a guide for research and input into the business case. Your outline might include the following sections:

- **Goals.** Describe your idea and what you hope to achieve, in terms of technology, market, or other relevant goals. If your idea is for a new product or service, explain how it differentiates your company from the competition and what makes this product or service difficult for competitors to imitate.

- **The expected benefits of the execution.** How will the idea, once it's made real, benefit customers or end users? Explain why your idea is an improvement over the status quo, and identify the potential competitive advantage it could give your company. Also discuss why this idea is a good fit for your company in terms of how it complements existing technology, strategic plans, manufacturing capabilities, or plans for future expansion. In some companies, you may need to demonstrate specific measurable improvements in costs, revenues, profit, or customer satisfaction.

- **Milestones.** List the major milestones you propose for the execution of your idea. In the interest of time, don't get caught up in describing the details of each step you'll take.

- **Potential obstacles and approaches for overcoming them.** Acknowledge possible problems or risks to show that you have considered them. Provide a plan of action for addressing these problems. For example, your customers may perceive your idea for consolidating project management and account representative roles into one department as a reduction in service. To counter this perception, you may develop a strategy for demonstrating how the change would actually improve their service.

- **A cost estimate for executing the innovation.** Include specific numbers wherever possible.

- **Resource requirements.** Identify the resources you'll need—people, equipment, budget, and so on. As appropriate, include details such as the number of people you would need and their areas of expertise.

Before anyone in a position to decide the fate of your idea attends a formal presentation or reviews your business case, they should already be favorably disposed to your idea. Get on the calendar of every critical decision maker. Brief them on your proposal, and ask for advice. If you are unable to address their questions immediately, do research to get the answers. Update your documents to reflect their input and acknowledge their contributions.

The format for a business case varies from company to company. As such, there is no correct length for a business case. The form and level of detail of your business case will vary depending on your idea and the expectations of the people who will read it.

For example, an idea to change juice packaging to make the product fit more easily into a refrigerator may require a presentation that outlines your market research, the cost of the new packaging, and estimated sales. A more significant change, such as introducing a new juice flavor, would likely require much more supporting documentation.

Creating multiple versions

Because the business case serves multiple purposes, you may want to consider creating at least two versions:

- A detailed plan that outlines the benefits, obstacles, and all of the action steps for distribution to the people responsible for implementing your idea.

- A less detailed version for use when presenting your idea to potential supporters. This plan should be succinct—your presentation should take about ten minutes—and it should clearly state the value of the innovation.

You may also want to craft a one-minute "elevator pitch"—four or five sentences that describe your innovation and the benefits it will create. This presentation can be used to get someone interested in your idea when you have limited time. Update these documents as you gather new information or gain insight into how to get people excited about your project.

Once you have created your business case, consider how you will present it to the stakeholders. What are their needs? What are their agendas? An innovation's success hinges on how well you know your stakeholders—and how well you can communicate your plan.

Steps for Building a Preliminary Business Case

1. **Make an outline.**

   Using your vision statement as a guide, make an outline of the topics you want to address in your business case. These could include goals, potential customers, the competition, the idea's expected benefits, a preliminary timeline, and cost and labor estimates. It's a good idea to include potential obstacles and how you will address them, because decision makers and stakeholders will most likely ask about anticipated problems.

2. **Fill in details where you can.**
   Work alone or with a group of people to document the information you already know for each topic in your outline. You may need to make estimates for topics such as profit projections, resource requirements, time frames, and costs. Be sure to note your assumptions. They may be challenged, so you'll need to be prepared to defend them.

3. **Gather data.**
   Gather data and do research to fill in the gaps in your business plan. Explore your assumptions to see whether you can find any facts that either support or undermine them. According to what you learn, update your business case. Remember that the process of building a business case is just as valuable as the document you create. By exploring the details of your project, you become an expert in what it is you're proposing.

4. **Ask for feedback.**
   Show your preliminary business case to trusted advisers and supporters in your informal network. Ask for advice on how to strengthen your case. Revise your document on the basis of the input you receive.

5. **"Presell" your idea.**
   Before anyone in a position to decide the fate of your idea attends a formal presentation or reviews your business case, they should already be favorably disposed to your idea. Arrange an informal

meeting with these people to ask for their advice on the ideas you have explored in your business case. Don't present them with the case at this point; just discuss it. You can then improve your document by incorporating the feedback you receive.

6. **Create multiple documents for different audiences.**
   Using the information you gather, create different versions of your document for different stakeholders.

   For example, you might want to have a detailed document for your team to use. You might want to prepare a higher-level slide presentation for communicating your idea to potential supporters. Also consider drafting an executive summary that highlights the major points in your case relevant to each stakeholder group. This short document will remind stakeholders of your proposed innovation's benefits and can facilitate a more specific discussion of your idea.

Step 5: Communicate with Your Stakeholders

YOUR SUCCESS IN GAINING support for your innovative idea will largely depend on your ability to influence various stakeholders. Before even building your business case, you will have identified your stakeholders and their interests and concerns regarding your innovation. This information will help you prepare a strategy for gaining each individual's support. Consider your strategy in terms of the person's level of involvement in the project, how that person might evaluate your idea, and their preferred means of communication.

Adapting your approach

To win support from various stakeholders, adapt your approach. For example:

- To get the support of your *vice president of finance*, you might prepare a formal presentation with extensive printed support materials such as cost estimates, industry spending trends, and the competitive advantage of your innovation.

- To gain the support of the *manufacturing manager whose department will have to implement your change*, you might use an entirely different approach. You might forgo the presentation and instead ask for an informal meeting. You might start the meeting by acknowledging how important the department is to the company and asking the manager to help you figure out how best to implement your idea. Consider explaining the benefits of your innovation and how it might make his employees' jobs easier in the long run.

"Selling" your idea

Your goal in communicating your idea is to influence your stakeholders to support your innovation. Essentially, you're "selling" the idea. When you describe your idea to each of your stakeholders, you will want to remember the acronym AIDA:

1. Generate *awareness* of your innovation.

2. Arouse *interest* in your ideas.

3. Create *desire* for your idea by demonstrating its benefits.

4. Ask for *action* to help implement your innovation successfully.

"One of the best ways to persuade others is with your ears— by listening to them."
—Dean Rusk

Tip: Does your idea complement an already successful initiative? If so, find people managing the other initiative, and explore ways to link your idea with theirs. By piggybacking in this way, you may be able to take advantage of pooled resources.

What Would YOU Do?

Don't Waste the Waste

E LLA IS A MARKETING manager at New Generation (New Gen), a midsize consumer foods company. She is concerned about the environment and is an avid recycler. Recently, she was surprised to learn that New Gen disposes of several tons of food waste every month at a local landfill.

New Gen uses consultants to monitor its environmental compliance with federal and state waste disposal regulations. Although New Gen is compliant, Ella believes there must be a better way to handle the waste. She discovers that if New Gen separated its waste into two streams, half of it could be sold to a local composting company and made into fertilizer. Ella calls the composting facility and learns that it is eager to get more high-quality waste—and has been seeking a new partner.

The timing seems perfect. Ella loves the idea because of its environmental benefits and wants to move quickly. She develops a vision statement and cultivates an informal network of supporters. She realizes she needs a sponsor since the idea she is promoting is not within the bounds of her job responsibility. So she informally recruits the vice president of community relations to act as her project sponsor. With the help of this sponsor, she drafts a business case. After garnering support from several midlevel managers, Ella is eager to move her idea forward. But she's uncertain what would be the best next step. Should she talk about her idea with key decision makers in upper management? Ask her sponsor to attend a meeting with her and present the idea to upper management? Identify all the key stakeholders she has yet to contact, and schedule meetings with them?

What would YOU do? The mentors will suggest a solution in *What You COULD Do.*

A presentation may be the best way to sell your idea. Some guiding principles to use when preparing a presentation include the following:

- **Identify the need for your project.** Describe the need for your project in terms of how it solves a recognized problem or helps exploit an important opportunity your audience can relate to.

- **Position your innovation.** Appeal to the needs, priorities, interests, and problems that are foremost in the mind of the person with whom you are communicating.

- **Use language that people can understand.** Strive for simplicity, and eliminate jargon wherever possible. Use examples that are relevant to your audience's needs.

- **Develop a unique value proposition for the audience.** Create a concise statement that powerfully conveys the essential benefits of your idea. Differentiate your idea from others by highlighting its advantages.

- **Have a clear idea of what you are asking of people.** Are you seeking their support? Do you need resources? People will want to know how you plan to involve them in your project.

- **Treat resistance and criticism as useful feedback.** Encourage people to provide feedback and voice concerns. You want to be able to understand concerns so you can address them directly. Explain that their input will help strengthen your project.

- **Use multiple forums.** Tailor the medium you use to communicate your idea to your audience. For example, you may choose individual informal meetings with some stakeholders, while more formal group presentations may be more appropriate for others.

Formalizing the project

As you communicate with stakeholders, work with your sponsor to identify the individuals whose approval will be necessary to continue with your project. Once you get the support of these decision makers, you will then be in a position to ask for the resources you need to formally execute your idea. These resources will likely include the people who will work on the idea and the funding to support their work.

At this point, your project may become formal enough to need a *project manager*. A project manager is a detail-oriented person who can help plan and coordinate the implementation of your idea. Typically, this person is skilled at navigating organizational processes. You may choose to assume this role yourself, or you may seek someone else to fill the role.

What You COULD Do.

Remember Ella's uncertainty about how best to move her idea about waste recycling forward?

Here's what the mentor suggests:

Before meeting with the decision makers, Ella needs to make sure she has identified *all* the important stakeholders and influencers—and developed a strategy for influencing them. Otherwise, she could jeopardize her project. In this case, the consultants are especially important because the decision makers will probably ask them for advice on Ella's idea. She knows that building support can require political finesse and a good understanding of the company as a whole. She has wisely asked her sponsor to help her develop a strategy for approaching *all* stakeholders and influencers before she seeks support from upper management.

At New Gen, upper management probably views the outside consultants as environmental experts and will ask them for advice on this issue. If Ella does not approach the consultants early, she runs the risk of their picking apart her idea in front of management, thereby diminishing her credibility. Ella should work with her sponsor to develop a strategy for communicating with all the important stakeholders and influencers before meeting with key decision makers—with or without her sponsor.

Step 6: Manage Resistance

NEW IDEAS OFTEN meet with resistance. Since innovations threaten the status quo, resistance is a normal reaction. For example, an R&D manager may be threatened by your idea for newly formulated house paint. She may see it as an encroachment on her territory. Or an engineering manager may view a new electronic time sheet as a nuisance, even though it may increase efficiency in the accounting department.

You will probably encounter two types of resistance: explicit and hidden. To be a successful innovation champion, you need to anticipate both types and be prepared to manage them. Tap your sponsors and other facilitators to help you develop a strategy to overcome both types of resistance.

Understanding explicit and hidden resistance

Explicit resistance comes in the form of open criticism. It is easier to manage because it is visible. Consider the idea to change the formula for house paint. You might hear that your innovation is:

- **Not needed in the marketplace or in the business.** "Our paint sells well, and customers report a high level of satisfaction. Why do we need a new formula?" or "Our process works perfectly well as it is. No change is needed."

- **Too risky.** "There are too many unknowns about how the new paint formula will work. We may lose customers if it's not as good as our current product."

- **Too expensive.** "We are already strapped for cash. We don't have money to invest in a new initiative."

- **Bound to fail.** "Two years ago we reformulated the Barn Red color to make it brighter. It was a total flop, and we lost a lot of customers."

- **Not technically feasible.** "The new formula cannot be manufactured to our quality standards. It won't hold up under extreme weather conditions."

Managing *hidden resistance* is a greater challenge. Since it is generally passive, it is more difficult to recognize. It often surfaces during the action phase of a project, such as when you are trying to mobilize the work group. People may miss deadlines, respond to requests late, or argue over allocation of time and resources among projects. Sometimes these incidents may occur for genuine reasons, but they may also indicate hidden resistance.

"There is nothing more difficult to carry out, nor more doubtful of success, nor more difficult to manage, than the creation of a new system."
—Niccolo Machiavelli

For example, you may have sought cost and price estimates for your new paint formula from executives in many departments, including manufacturing, sales, and R&D. While these people may have seemed positive about the project in your initial meetings, they may drag their feet once you try to execute it. You will then have to identify the cause of this hidden resistance and deal with it effectively to make progress.

Tip: Create and show drawings, prototypes, models, or other proof-of-concept tools to give people a concrete idea of what your innovation looks like.

Identifying causes of resistance

A prominent person who opposes your innovative idea can easily derail your effort. Therefore, the first step is to determine whether the person is a critical stakeholder or can influence an important decision maker. If the person is not going to be involved in any way in your project, you may be able to ignore his or her objections. In most cases, however, you will need to address people's concerns to get them to work toward your idea's implementation.

Resistance is not usually a problem in itself; it is a symptom of an underlying issue. Typically, it can be caused by the following:

- Fear of the unknown

- A belief that the innovation is not necessary

- Personality conflicts

- The desire to protect oneself from risk or uncertainty

- An assessment or understanding of an opportunity that differs from yours

- Lack of rewards for innovating or accepting change

- Fear of disruption of organizational order or company culture

- Concern about workload or available resources

If you can identify the cause of the resistance, you'll be in a better position to directly address it. For example, the R&D manager who says that your new paint formula is not technically sound may really think the materials you've suggested using will not stand up to testing. Or perhaps the reason for her resistance is less obvious. For instance, she might be trying to protect her credibility. She may feel insecure because you, as an outsider, have identified a potentially better way of doing things. Knowing that insecurity is at the root of her resistance can help you develop a strategy for winning her acceptance. Sit down with her and acknowledge her expertise in this area. Ask her to explain her concerns, and see whether she has any advice for how to improve on your idea. Find the valuable part of her criticism and thank her for her help.

Participation can help overcome opposition. If you continue to involve this manager by seeking her opinion as you proceed, there is a good chance she will start to see herself as part of your support system—and may feel more secure about the project.

Overcoming resistance

There are many means available for dealing with resistance to your innovation. The table "Tactics for overcoming resistance" provides examples.

Tactics for overcoming resistance

Tactic	Method	Example
Persuasion	• Use data, evidence, facts and logic. • Communicate the features and benefits of your idea.	If the sales director resists your new paint formula because she fears that you may lose customers, review your market and product research with her. Highlight the benefits. Will this formula generate less waste, thereby appealing to an environmentally conscious consumer? Will it cost less than your current formula? Show her the need for this product, and try to convince her that customers will respond positively.
Participation	• Involve the person by asking for ideas or other contributions to the project. • Share ownership or credit for your idea or its implementation with this person. • Thank this person for his assistance, and acknowledge his efforts in front of managers and other influential people.	The head of purchasing might feel threatened by your suggestion to change the company's supply chain management system. Try to get him involved in your project early. Ask for his advice. Give him credit for his good ideas in group meetings to feel more involved.

Tactic	Method	Example
Facilitation	• Provide skills training and other forms of transition support to help the person feel less overwhelmed. • Help those affected adversely by the innovation to adapt to it. • Obtain the additional resources necessary to make the person more comfortable with your idea.	An idea to restructure the sales team to focus on industry sectors may mean extra work for salespeople while they become experts in areas they know little about. Make it your responsibility to help them with training or other resources to facilitate their acceptance of the innovation. Look for opportunities to help them learn quickly so that they can focus on the selling process.
Negotiation	• Identify the aspects of the project that are of concern, and explore possible alternatives that address the source of the resistance. • Make compromises or trade-offs in the design or implementation of your idea.	If manufacturing says your formula is hard to make to its quality standards, explore alternative formulations or materials that will address its concerns, and modify the paint accordingly.
Direction	• Use power or authority to ask that something be done. Exercise your power, or seek the authority of a high-level supporter or sponsor.	After the completion of your pilot project, you ask a team member to report on his findings by the following week. Three weeks later, this person has yet to deliver any results. It may be time for someone in upper management to emphasize the importance of your project and its high priority.

Be prepared to encounter resistance throughout your project. Keep a clear head and continue to focus on your vision. Maintaining a positive attitude and recognizing that all innovators have to overcome obstacles along the way will help you stay the course and successfully carry out your idea.

"Innovative accomplishments . . . generally involve acquiring and using power and influence."

—Rosabeth Moss Kanter

Steps for Overcoming Resistance

1. **Listen attentively to all feedback.**

   Pay attention when people criticize your idea. Ask probing questions to get at the heart of their concerns.

   For example, you might ask, "Can you tell me more about that?" "Can you share with me the facts that support your opinion?" Often those who criticize are aware of something that you can't see. Their honest feedback may help you strengthen your plan or improve the way you present your idea.

2. **Consider your critic's role and reputation.**

   If the criticism does not seem to be constructive, work with your sponsor or other advisers to evaluate the person's importance. Is the person opposing your idea essential to its successful implementation? Is he someone who can influence others or who controls resources you need to implement your idea? Do you need his support to continue? If the answer to any of these questions is yes, you may need to devise a strategy to overcome the resistance. If the person is viewed as a chronic complainer, however, you may not need to win his support.

3. **Identify the cause of the resistance.**

   Consider why this person opposes your idea. Is the resistance due to some shortcoming of the idea itself or due to how it impacts this person? Is she feeling threatened? Is she apprehensive about the risks? Is she too busy to take on more responsibility and afraid that you may ask her to contribute to your project? Is she concerned that she will no longer be needed when the project is complete? You may want to ask your sponsor or someone who is removed from the project to help you identify the cause(s) of resistance.

4. **Develop a strategy to manage resistance.**

   On the basis of what you know about the person and the likely cause(s) of resistance, decide on an approach to manage resistance. If risk is his concern, consider trying to persuade him with facts and logic as to how you will mitigate or manage the elements of risk. If he seems threatened by the project, encourage his participation by asking for advice and inviting him to meetings. Other tactics you might consider include providing training to make the person feel less overwhelmed, offering the person something in exchange for his support, providing more data to support your proposal, or simply directing the person to complete the task at hand.

5. **Continue to build a large support network.**

   Recognize that you might not be able to convince everyone to support your project. However, the more people who support you, the more likely you are to overcome other opponents.

Step 7: Stay Passionate About Your Innovation

A FINAL KEY STEP IN ensuring successful execution of a new idea is to maintain your own enthusiasm—as well as others'—for the project. Understanding the challenge of keeping up momentum and reviewing strategies for sustaining enthusiasm can help you with this crucial step.

Understanding the momentum challenge

Innovations take time to carry out, and maintaining momentum for your project will likely prove difficult. It is much easier to get people excited over a vision at the beginning of a project than it is to maintain enthusiasm during the day-to-day progress toward your goal. You must sustain people's motivation to reach the goal by being a passionate and persistent advocate yourself.

As your project moves from planning to execution, you need to actively support your team, reassure the people who will be affected by any changes, and keep the stakeholders who control the resources you need informed of your progress.

"Successful innovation is not a feat of intellect, but a feat of will."
—Joseph Schumpeter

Sustaining enthusiasm for your idea

To keep your team and stakeholders motivated throughout your innovation's implementation, consider the following techniques for maintaining momentum:

- **Deliver on your promises.** Successful innovators under-promise and overdeliver. Don't make promises you aren't sure you can keep.

- **Meet deadlines.** Set realistic deadlines. Meeting deadlines demonstrates that your team is moving forward smoothly and is capable of implementing the entire project. If you miss a deadline, people may wonder whether there are serious problems with your project or whether the team lacks commitment.

- **Provide benefits early.** Look for ways to show the value of your project early—for example, at an early stage in the development of a new internal process.

- **Focus on short-term wins.** Set goals for yourself that you can achieve quickly. Once you achieve a goal, advertise your success. Small victories lend credibility to your overall innovation plan and build the morale of people on your implementation team.

- **Keep your supporters informed.** Once you get people's support, continue to update them on your progress. Plan to make frequent presentations to top management. You want influential people to maintain a high level of interest so they continue to view your project as relevant and important.

- **Motivate your team.** Many people concentrate on completing their routine activities, leaving work on special projects for slow times. If you ask people to increase their workload to help with your innovation, foot dragging or inactivity is a constant danger. Meet with your project team regularly and consider circulating weekly status reports to keep everyone up-to-date.

- **Keep a low profile when you are vulnerable.** Prepare for problems that will surface during the project, and quietly work to solve them. Give yourself time to show progress. Once you have achieved a milestone or solved a problem, resurface and draw attention to your project.

As your project progresses, remember to be patient. It may take several months or even years to fully execute your innovation. Remind yourself that throughout history innovation champions have had to be persistent—and passionate—to get their ideas adopted.

Tip: When you enter the action phase of the project, make sure that the people who will be doing the work have the support tools, time, and training necessary to implement your idea. People will be more inclined to buy into the work if they feel well trained and prepared.

Tips and Tools

Tools for
Executing Innovation

Could You Be an Innovation Champion?

Think of an innovative idea you've recently learned about.
Write the idea in the space below, then answer yes or no for each question.

Innovation You're Considering Championing:

Do You Have ...	Yes	No
1. A strong conviction about the merits of and need for this innovation?		
2. A strong sense of ownership of the innovation, even if it originated with someone else?		
3. An overpowering desire to get the innovation accepted and put into action?		
4. A willingness to commit time, energy, and other personal resources over an extended period of time, well beyond the demands of your formal job description, to promote the innovation?		
5. A willingness to experience negative reactions and setbacks as you try to execute the innovation?		
Total		

Interpreting your score: if you answered yes to most of these questions, you're on the road to becoming an innovation champion! This book helps you turn your innovation into reality in spite of the skeptics, the setbacks, and the obstacles you'll encounter along the way.

Crafting a Vision Statement

Use this worksheet to draft a vision statement to share with others.
See "Steps for Developing Your Vision" for help with envisioning the idea
that you will record in your vision statement.

Description of Idea:

Briefly describe your idea. Do you have a name for the idea or project?

Idea Assessment:

Does your idea address a perceived need or solve a problem? If so, what is it? If not, you may want to revisit your idea.

Users or Customers:

List the end users or customers for this innovation.

Benefits:

List the key benefits that make this idea worth pursuing. For example, will it lead to larger markets and growth, increase profits, or make your organization more efficient?

Draft Vision Statement:

Using the information you have recorded above, draft a preliminary vision statement. Start with a short paragraph. Since the goal is to stir up enthusiasm for your idea, describe your goals vividly. Be sure that your statement clearly and concisely communicates your idea and appeals to your stakeholders' interests.

Feedback:

Once you have a preliminary statement, ask some close friends or colleagues for feedback. Record the responses you receive here.

Revised Statement:

Now, revise your vision statement based on the feedback you receive.

How Good Is Your Vision Statement?

Your objective is to articulate your vision to the people who can help you make your idea a reality. Once you have the vision in your mind's eye, you will want to translate it to a format that can be communicated with impact to others. While some vision statements begin with words, others may use some sort of visual aid, like a sketch or a model. Think of the innovation you identified in the table "Could you be an innovation champion?" Write a vision statement in the space provided below, and then answer each question with "yes" or "no."

Vision Statement:

Does Your Vision Statement . . .	Yes	No
1. **Describe your desired outcome vividly?** A vision becomes truly powerful when people can understand its goals and direction. Try to craft a statement that helps others "see" the future outcome in their mind's eye.		
2. **Appeal to stakeholders' needs and interests?** Your statement should appeal to the implicit or explicit interests of your stakeholders.		
3. **Stir up enthusiasm?** You will need to gain support for your idea to recruit a team. Convey your vision with excitement to stimulate enthusiasm in others.		
4. **Communicate effectively?** Strive to create a clear vision that you can describe to others within two minutes. Imagine that you have someone's attention for only the length of an elevator ride. How would you explain your vision?		
Total		

Interpreting your results: if you answered yes to all four questions, your vision statement will likely be very effective. If you answered no to any questions, think about ways you might strengthen your vision statement.

Communicating with a Stakeholder

The support of stakeholders is critical to the implementation of your idea.
Use this form to prepare for meetings with stakeholders. Complete one form
for each stakeholder. After your meeting, use the form "Managing
Communications Follow-up" to identify your next steps.

Part I : Your Stakeholder

Identify your stakeholder.
Who is she? What is her title? What are her key responsibilities?

How will this stakeholder view your innovation?
For example, how does the idea impact her power, status, work schedule, etc.? How does this idea benefit her? List the benefits and disadvantages in the table below.

Benefits	Disadvantages
Example: A change in the process will enable her employees to produce 10 more circuit boards per shift.	*Example: A change in the process will eliminate the need for one assembly-line worker per shift.*

Part II : Your Communication Approach

Where will you meet?
Should the meeting be on neutral territory? In a conference room? In your office?

What is the specific objective you want to accomplish in your meeting?
Are you asking for support, advice, or buy-in?

How are you going to influence this person?
For example, what benefits for her and/or the company will you emphasize?

How will you present your idea?
Will you present your idea using visual aids, drawings, and/or prototypes? What backup data will you use—for example, research or marketing reports?

Managing Communications Follow-up

After you meet with a stakeholder, you should develop a follow-up strategy.
Use this form to track your progress in winning the support of your stakeholders.
Use it in conjunction with the "Communicating with a Stakeholder" form and,
if applicable, with the worksheet "Overcoming Resistance."

Contact Name: **Contact Role:**

Meeting Date:

Proposed Innovation:

Questions They Asked:

Feedback You Received:

Positive	Negative

Meeting Outcome:

Use the space below to indicate what you accomplished in the meeting or any problems that surfaced.

For example, did the person support your idea or show resistance? Did you set an expectation that you would follow up? If so, how?

Next Steps:

List the actions you will take and record the date you want to complete them.

For example, will you meet with the person again? Should you provide the person with supporting documents? Do you need to follow up on any questions? If so, when?

Action	Completion Date

Overcoming Resistance

Use this tool to diagnose the cause of resistance and plan how you might overcome it.

Part I: Identifying Resistance

Name:

How has the resistance been expressed?
For example, has the person said in a meeting that your idea will never work or said that it is too risky? Has he refused to complete a task you asked of him?

Is this person critical to the success of your project?
For example, does he control resources you will need? Is he likely to influence other important decision makers? Do you need him to work directly on your implementation?

What do you think might be the underlying cause(s) of the resistance?
Are there legitimate reasons for this person to resist the idea, such as high cost or risk? Or does he feel threatened by the idea? Is he generally opposed to changing the status quo?

Part II: Identifying Tactics to Overcome Resistance

Answer yes, no, or unsure to help identify a strategy for approaching this person.

Statement	Yes	No	Unsure
1. I need this person's ideas, skills, or information to improve my project.			
2. This person needs to have a sense of ownership in this project for it to succeed.			
3. I am open to sharing credit or control with this person.			

*If you answered yes to at least two of the statements on the previous page, you might want to consider using the **participation** tactic. To use this tactic effectively, you could:*

• *Involve the person by asking for ideas or other contributions to the project.*
• *Share ownership or credit for your idea or its implementation with this person.*

Statement	Yes	No	Unsure
4. My proposal will probably cause a major inconvenience to this person or to the people who work for her.			
5. This person or the people who work for him will need training or other support to implement my idea.			
6. The status quo is probably more appealing to this person than the idea of initiating a change.			

*If you answered yes to at least two of the statements above, you might want to consider using the **facilitation** tactic. To use this tactic effectively, you could:*

• *Provide the skills needed.*
• *Provide training and other forms of transition support to help the person feel less overwhelmed.*

Statement	Yes	No	Unsure
7. This person tends to make decisions based on reason, not on emotion.			
8. This person does not appear to feel threatened by my idea.			
9. This person is probably not aware of the details of the innovation and the potential benefits it will have.			

*If you answered yes to at least two of the statements above, you might want to consider using the **persuasion** tactic. To use this tactic effectively, you could:*

• *Use data, evidence, facts, and logic.*
• *Communicate the features and benefits of your idea.*

Statement	Yes	No	Unsure
10. In exchange for this person's support, I am willing to modify the idea or its implementation.			
11. This person has a reputation for being able to work through differences to find a solution.			
12. I have something (e.g., resources) that this person needs for another project.			

*If you answered yes to at least two of the statements on the previous page, you might want to consider using the **negotiation** tactic. To use this tactic effectively, you could:*

• *Identify the aspects of the project that are of concern and possible alternatives.*
• *Make compromises or trade-offs in the design or implementation of your idea.*

Statement	Yes	No	Unsure
13. I need this person to complete a task or to provide resources for my project.			
14. I have the authority to tell this person that she needs to do something, or I have a strong supporter who has that level of authority.			
15. Expectations of rewards or disciplinary action are likely to motivate this person to do what I need him or her to do.			

*If you answered yes to at least two of the statements above, you might want to consider using the **direction** tactic. To use this tactic effectively, you could:*

• *Use your power or authority to ask that something be done.*
• *Seek the authority of a high-level supporter or sponsor to ask that something be done.*

Please note: if you scored within the suggested range for multiple tactics, consider using more than one approach, according to what you know about the person's work style and personality.

Test Yourself

This section offers ten multiple-choice questions to help you identify your baseline knowledge of the essentials of executing innovation. Answers to the questions are given at the end of the test.

1. Which of the following is the *best* way to approach a potential sponsor about your innovative idea?

- a. "Do you have a few minutes to discuss a great new idea I have? I would really like your support in moving it forward."
- b. "Do you have a few minutes to discuss an idea I have? I am curious to see whether you think it is worth pursuing."
- c. "Do you have a few minutes to discuss an idea I have? I'd like your advice on how to move it forward."

2. When should you approach an important decision maker for support for your innovative idea?

- a. Once you have crafted a compelling vision statement and recruited a high-level sponsor.
- b. Once you have crafted a compelling vision statement, recruited a high-level sponsor, and built an informal network of supporters.
- c. Once you have crafted a compelling vision statement, recruited a high-level sponsor, built an informal network of supporters, and achieved some short-term wins.

3. Which of the following is an example of how an innovator *failed* to recognize the evaluation criteria that her stakeholders would probably use to assess her idea?

a. The innovator made a presentation to the manufacturing department about how her new vacuum cleaner could leverage the excellent manufacturing processes already in place in the factory and could cut down on the need for forced overtime to meet delivery demands.

b. The innovator made a presentation to potential customers about all the internal features of her new vacuum cleaner that made it cheaper to build.

c. The innovator made a presentation to the sales team about how they could promise to deliver more vacuum cleaners to their customers because of the speed with which her new design could be built.

4. As you develop an idea for a new feature for your company's best-selling software program, why would it be important to recruit a gatekeeper to help with your project?

a. To help develop a strategy for presenting your ideas more effectively to management and to work behind the scenes to build support.

b. To provide technical advice and to connect you with other people who can help you with information, expertise, or other resources.

c. To lend credibility to your venture and to accelerate acceptance of your new idea by important decision makers.

5. Which of the following is the best vision statement?

a. "By standardizing our product and eliminating custom options, we will increase our earnings by 20 percent. We will build Web sites more quickly than our competitors and will leverage our years of design experience to create the best templates available."

b. "Standardization is our future. Without it, we will fail. We will provide the highest-quality, quickest-to-build, and easiest-to-maintain Web sites to our customers. Our design experience and technical expertise will differentiate us."

c. "We need to reduce the time we spend building Web sites in order to beat the competition. Otherwise, we can't survive in this market. Template-based Web sites will help us achieve our goal. Everyone will be asked to give extra effort over the next two months to design templates while completing current projects. But once we have a library of templates, we will be more productive, better able to meet our customers' aggressive schedules, and make money while we're at it!"

6. Decide whether the following statement is true or false: the best person to champion an idea is the person who thought of it.

a. True.

b. False.

7. Which of the following would *not* be addressed in an outline for a business case?

    a. A detailed breakdown of each of the steps you will take to achieve your goals.

    b. Specific resources you will need to achieve your goals.

    c. Estimated costs you will incur to achieve your goals.

8. You sense that your company's warehouse supervisor is resisting your idea for a new distribution system because he feels overwhelmed by the role he will have to play in its execution. Which of the following would be the best tactic to try to influence him to accept your idea?

    a. Direction.

    b. Participation.

    c. Facilitation.

9. Which of the following might *undermine* your team's enthusiasm for your idea as your project progresses?

    a. Demonstrating benefits to stakeholders as early as possible.

    b. Keeping a steady focus on your long-term goals.

    c. Circulating weekly status reports to everyone on the project team.

10. Why is it important to determine what specific help or support you will need from stakeholders *before* meeting with them?

a. People won't oppose your idea if you ask them for specific help or support.

b. People want to know how you plan to involve them in your project.

c. Asking for a specific type of help or support makes people understand the need for your project.

Answers to test questions

1, c. Most people are willing to give you a few minutes of their time to discuss a new idea. By asking for advice instead of support, you engage the person in the development of the idea without making her feel that she has to commit to it immediately. At the early stages of your project, it is probably too soon for the person to objectively form an opinion on whether your idea is good or bad. After the person has had time to consider the merits of your idea—and decides that it is worth pursuing—you may be able to ask for help in developing a strategy for moving it forward and for getting support. The very process of being asked for help or advice creates a sense of ownership that can make this person want to be your sponsor.

2, b. Effective idea champions *identify* the decision makers who will affect the success of their innovations early on, but they wait to *approach* them for support. They test their ideas on others first, and seek the decision makers' support only after they have built a support network among peers and colleagues. However, waiting *too* long can often be as problematic as approaching someone too early. Your sponsor should be able to help you identify the appropriate time to approach the decision makers whose support you will need to ensure the success of your project.

3, b. In this case, the innovator didn't show the customers how her product would benefit *them*. A good strategy for influencing stakeholders is to consider how your idea can provide benefits to that particular person. Successful ideas benefit different stakeholders in different ways. Describing features that make the vacuum cleaner easier to build doesn't address customers' needs; therefore, the innovator's presentation didn't provide a compelling reason for customers to choose it over another brand.

4, b. A gatekeeper is usually an expert in a functional area or subject. In this case, you would probably seek a software engineer who is up-to-date in her knowledge of the field and can serve as a useful sounding board and information resource. Good gatekeepers have extensive contacts within and outside your organization, so they can connect you with other people who can help you with information, expertise, or other resources.

5, c. This statement clearly describes the direction the company will take and outlines why this new direction is necessary. It acknowledges the potential sacrifices people will have to make, but makes clear that the rewards will be worth the efforts.

6, b. A common misconception is that the person who generates an idea should be the person to execute it. Often, the person who dreams up an idea is great at thinking creatively and identifying solutions to difficult problems. However, he often has neither the skills nor the temperament to bring his idea to fruition. An *innovation champion* has the know-how, energy, daring, dedication, and perseverance that are needed to turn an idea into reality. While many people in an organization can generate creative ideas, few people commit to putting ideas into action. When the idea creator also has the skills and interest to promote and implement his idea, he can be an effective champion, but this should not be taken for granted in every situation.

7, a. You do *not* want to get caught up in project management specifics when crafting your business case. Include only the major milestones that illustrate progress toward your goals, not each step along the way. You can provide execution details later, after the business case has generated interest in your project.

8, c. Facilitation helps those who are likely to be affected adversely by the innovation to adapt to it. Providing training, skill building, and other forms of transitional support will likely help the supervisor feel less overwhelmed by the tasks involved in executing your idea.

9, b. Focusing exclusively on your long-term goals may not keep people motivated. In order to maintain momentum and enthusiasm, you need to concentrate on short-term wins. Set goals for your team that can be achieved quickly—and be sure to advertise your success!

10, b. By clearly identifying your objectives before you meet with each stakeholder (Do you want resources from him? Support from her?), you show why the person's involvement is important, and you make it clear what you are asking for. Otherwise, you may get a nod of acceptance, but no concrete support when you need it.

To Learn More

Articles

Hamel, Gary. "The Why, What, and How of Management Innovation." *Harvard Business Review* OnPoint Enhanced Edition, February 2006.

Few companies have been able to come up with a formal process for fostering management innovation. Four components can help: a big problem that demands fresh thinking, creative principles, or paradigms that can reveal new approaches; an evaluation of the conventions that constrain novel thinking; and examples and analogies that help redefine what can be done. No doubt, existing management processes in your organization exacerbate the big problems you're hoping to solve. After documenting these details, ask the people involved with the process to weigh in. This exploration may reveal opportunities to reinvent your management processes. A management innovation, the author says, creates long-lasting advantage when it meets at least one of three conditions: it is based on a novel principle that challenges the orthodoxy; it is systemic, involving a range of processes and methods; or it is part of a program of invention, where progress compounds over time.

Hering, Dean, and Jeffrey Phillips. "Innovate on Purpose." *Harvard Management Update*, September 2006.

More than ever before, companies need to innovate to grow. Yet all too often, innovation is accidental rather than intentional. Dean Hering and Jeffrey Phillips—chief innovator and vice president of sales and marketing, respectively, at Raleigh, North Carolina-based OVO, a division of NetCentrics that offers services and software to reduce innovation cycle time—have developed a four-step methodology to aid companies that seek growth through innovation. This article outlines their sustainable, repeatable approach to innovation and addresses the logistics of new product launches after development of those innovations.

Kanter, Rosabeth Moss. "The Middle Manager as Innovator." *Harvard Business Review* OnPoint Enhanced Edition, September 2001.

Kanter's study of 165 effective middle managers in five leading corporations explores creative managerial contributions and the conditions that stimulate innovation. This article points out that enterprising, entrepreneurial middle managers share a number of characteristics: comfort with change, clarity of direction, thoroughness, a participative management style, as well as persuasiveness, persistence, and discretion.

Krackhardt, David, and Jeffrey R. Hanson. "Informal Networks: The Company Behind the Chart." *Harvard Business Review*, July–August 1993.

A formal organizational chart won't reveal which people confer on technical matters or discuss office politics over lunch.

Much of the real work in any company gets done through an informal organization, with complex networks of relationships that cross functions and divisions. According to the authors, managers can harness the power in their companies by learning more about the advice network, which reveals the people to whom others turn to get work done; the trust network, which uncovers who shares delicate information; and the communication network, which shows who talks about work-related matters.

Laduke, Patty, Tom Andrews, and Keith Yamashita. "Igniting a Passion for Innovation." *Strategy & Innovation*, July–August 2003.

Innovation necessitates change, and there are often powerful emotional barriers to change. In this article, the authors describe how even the most brilliant innovation efforts can fall flat if you neglect to convey the why behind the what. By beginning with a compelling purpose that addresses your audience's emotional and intellectual needs in equal measure, you can capture people's hearts and minds—and ignite a passion for innovation. If you can't inspire your team with a sense of purpose, you'll never see your vision come to life.

Levitt, Theodore. "Creativity Is Not Enough." *Harvard Business Review* OnPoint Enhanced Edition, August 2002.

Creativity is often touted as a miraculous road to organizational growth and affluence. But creative new ideas can hinder rather than help a company if they are put forward irresponsibly. In this article, the author, a professor emeritus at Harvard

Business School and a former *Harvard Business Review* editor, offers suggestions for the person with a great new idea. First, work with the situation as it is—recognize that the executive is already bombarded with problems. Second, act responsibly by including in your proposal at least a minimal indication of the costs, risks, manpower, and time your idea may involve.

Books

Kotter, John P. *Leading Change*. Boston: Harvard Business School Press, 1996.

In this book, the author examines the efforts of more than one hundred companies to remake themselves into better competitors. He identifies the most common mistakes leaders and managers make in attempting to create change, and offers an eight-step process to overcome the obstacles and carry out the firm's agenda: establishing a greater sense of urgency, creating the guiding coalition, developing a vision and strategy, communicating the change vision, empowering others to act, creating short-term wins, consolidating gains and producing even more change, and institutionalizing new approaches in the future.

Pinchot, Gifford, III. *Intrapreneuring: Why You Don't Have to Leave the Corporation to Become an Entrepreneur*. New York: Harper & Row, 1985.

In this book, Gifford Pinchot illustrates his concept of "intrapreneuring," or how an employee within a large corporation, using courage, foresight, and tools for managing the corporate immune system, can succeed in taking direct, entrepreneur-like responsibility for turning an idea into a profitable product or service. Pinchot provides a blueprint for how an individual can become an intrapreneur and how companies can develop their employees' intrapreneurial talents. The author shows potential intrapreneurs—whether managers or staff—how to choose an idea, get it approved, find the necessary funds, and make the project succeed.

Pinchot, Gifford, and Ron Pellman. *Intrapreneuring in Action: A Handbook for Business Innovation*. San Francisco: Berrett-Koehler, 1999.

A follow-up to 1995's *Intrapreneuring*, this hands-on guide shows how to create a climate of innovation that brings out the entrepreneurial spirit of an organization. In this book, Pinchot and Pellman describe sixteen proven "Rules of Intrapreneuring in Action" and show how to apply these rules to all kinds of innovation, from new products and services and better ways of relating to customers to smarter approaches to globalization.

eLearning Programs

Harvard Business School Publishing. *Case in Point*. Boston: Harvard Business School Publishing, 2004.

Case in Point is a flexible set of online cases, designed to help prepare middle- and senior-level managers for a variety of leadership challenges. These short, reality-based scenarios provide sophisticated content to create a focused view into the realities of the life of a leader. Your managers will experience Aligning Strategy, Removing Implementation Barriers, Overseeing Change, Anticipating Risk, Ethical Decisions, Building a Business Case, Cultivating Customer Loyalty, Emotional Intelligence, Developing a Global Perspective, Fostering Innovation, Defining Problems, Selecting Solutions, Managing Difficult Interactions, The Coach's Role, Delegating for Growth, Managing Creativity, Influencing Others, Managing Performance, Providing Feedback, and Retaining Talent.

Harvard Business School Publishing. *Managing Change.* Boston: Harvard Business School Publishing, 2000.

According to leadership experts, 70 percent of all corporate change initiatives fail. This interactive program combines the theory and research of five change strategists to quickly and easily help managers balance pace and roll out change initiatives successfully. Managers will learn the numerous phases of change, critical mistakes to avoid, how to initiate carefully paced periods of smaller change, and how to lead successfully through change. Lessons include how to: balance content, processes, and employees' emotions during a change initiative; maintain continuous change without tearing the organization apart (dynamic stability); navigate the phases of a change process; and utilize empowered employees and trust to support a change effort.

Harvard Business School Publishing. *What Is a Leader?* Boston: Harvard Business School Publishing, 2001.

This interactive program helps managers apply concepts and grow from a competent manager to an exceptional leader. Use this program to assess your ability to lead your organization through fundamental change, evaluate your leadership skills by examining how you allocate your time, and analyze your "emotional intelligence" to determine your strengths and weaknesses as a leader. In addition, work through interactive, real-world scenarios to determine what approach to take when diagnosing problems, how to manage and even use the stress associated with change, empower others, and practice empathy when managing the human side of interactions. Based on the research and writings of John Kotter, author of *Leading Change*, and other of today's top leadership experts, this program is essential study for anyone charged with setting the direction of—and providing the motivation for—a modern organization.

Sources for Executing Innovation

The following sources aided in development of this book:

Kanter, Rosabeth Moss. "The Middle Manager as Innovator." *Harvard Business Review* OnPoint Enhanced Edition, September 2001.

Kotter, John P. *Leading Change*. Boston: Harvard Business School Press, 1996.

Krackhardt, David, and Jeffrey R. Hanson. "Informal Networks: The Company Behind the Chart." *Harvard Business Review*, July–August 1993.

Laduke, Patty, Tom Andrews, and Keith Yamashita. "Igniting a Passion for Innovation." *Strategy & Innovation*, July–August 2003.

Levitt, Theodore. "Creativity Is Not Enough." *Harvard Business Review* OnPoint Enhanced Edition, August 2002.

Nochur, Kumar. *Skills for Innovators*. Newton, MA: Vidya Inc., 2003.

Pinchot, Gifford, III. *Intrapreneuring: Why You Don't Have to Leave the Corporation to Become an Entrepreneur*. New York: Harper & Row, 1985.

Pinchot, Gifford, III, and Ron Pellman. *Intrapreneuring in Action: A Handbook for Business Innovation*. San Francisco: Berrett-Koehler, 1999.

Notes

Notes

Notes

Notes

Notes

Notes

Notes

How to Order

Harvard Business Press publications are available worldwide from your local bookseller or online retailer.

You can also call:
1-800-668-6780

Our product consultants are available to help you 8:00 a.m.–6:00 p.m., Monday–Friday, Eastern Time. Outside the U.S. and Canada, call: 617-783-7450.

Please call about special discounts for quantities greater than ten.

You can order online at:
www.HBSPress.org